D0430113

altar
ego

Also by Craig Groeschel

STUDY GUIDE

FIVE SESSIONS

Becoming Who God Says You Are

altar ego

CRAIG GROESCHEL

with Christine M. Anderson

ZONDERVAN®

ZONDERVAN.com/
AUTHORTRACKER
follow your favorite authors

ZONDERVAN

Altar Ego Study Guide
Copyright © 2013 by Craig Groeschel

This title is also available as a Zondervan ebook. Visit www.zondervan.com/ebooks.

Requests for information should be addressed to:

Zondervan, *Grand Rapids, Michigan 49530*

ISBN 978-0-310-89494-0

All Scripture quotations, unless otherwise indicated, are taken from The Holy Bible, *New International Version®, NIV®.* Copyright © 1973, 1978, 1984, 2011 by Biblica, Inc.™ Used by permission. All rights reserved worldwide.

Scripture quotations marked CEV are taken from the *Contemporary English Version.* Copyright © 1995 by American Bible Society. Used by permission.

Scripture quotations marked ESV are taken from *The Holy Bible, English Standard Version,* copyright © 2001 by Crossway Bibles, a division of Good News Publishers. Used by permission. All rights reserved.

Scripture quotations marked KNOX are taken from the Knox Bible. Copyright © 2012 Westminster Diocese. Published by Barionus Press. All rights reserved.

Scripture quotations marked MSG are taken from *The Message.* Copyright © 1993, 1994, 1995, 1996, 2000, 2001, 2002. Used by permission of NavPress Publishing Group.

Scripture quotations marked NLT are taken from the *Holy Bible, New Living Translation,* copyright © 1996, 2004. Used by permission of Tyndale House Publishers, Inc., Wheaton, Illinois. All rights reserved.

Any Internet addresses (websites, blogs, etc.) and telephone numbers in this book are offered as a resource. They are not intended in any way to be or imply an endorsement by Zondervan, nor does Zondervan vouch for the content of these sites and numbers for the life of this book.

All rights reserved. No part of this publication may be reproduced, stored in a retrieval system, or transmitted in any form or by any means — electronic, mechanical, photocopy, recording, or any other — except for brief quotations in printed reviews, without the prior permission of the publisher.

Craig Groeschel is represented by Thomas J. Winters and Jeffrey C. Durm of Winters, King & Associates, Inc., Tulsa, Oklahoma.

Cover design: Jason Gabbert Design
Interior design: David Conn

Printed in the United States of America

13 14 15 16 17 18 19 20 /DCI/ 20 19 18 17 16 15 14 13 12 11 10 9 8 7 6 5 4 3 2

CONTENTS

HOW TO USE THIS GUIDE

Group Size

The *Altar Ego* video curriculum is designed to be experienced in a group setting such as a Bible study, Sunday school class, or any small group gathering. To ensure everyone has enough time to participate in discussions, it is recommended that large groups break up into smaller groups of four to six people each.

Materials Needed

Each participant should have his or her own Study Guide, which includes notes for video segments, directions for activities and discussion questions, as well as personal studies to deepen learning between sessions.

Timing

The time notations — for example (17 minutes) — indicate the *actual* time of video segments and the *suggested* times for each activity or discussion. For example:

Individual Activity: **What I Want to Remember** (2 Minutes)

Adhering to the suggested times will enable you to complete each session in one hour. If you have a longer meeting, you may wish to allow more time for discussion and activities. You may also opt to devote two meetings rather than one to each session. In addition to allowing discussions to be more spacious, this has the added advantage of allowing group members to read related chapters in the *Altar Ego* book and to complete the personal study between meetings. In the second meeting, devote the time allotted for watching the video to discussing group members' insights and questions from their reading and personal study.

Facilitation

Each group should appoint a facilitator who is responsible for starting the video and for keeping track of time during discussions and activities. Facilitators may also read questions aloud and monitor discussions, prompting participants to respond and assuring that everyone has the opportunity to participate.

Personal Studies

Maximize the impact of the curriculum with additional study between group sessions. Every personal study includes reflection questions, Bible study, and a guided prayer activity. You'll get the most out of the curriculum by setting aside about one hour between sessions for personal study. For each session, you may wish to complete the personal study all in one sitting or to spread it out over a few days.

OVERCOMING THE LABELS THAT BIND YOU

World conditions are constantly at work eroding the high profile specifics of each person into a flat and featureless generality, identified by label: Introvert, Elder Material, Ectomorph, Unsaved, Anorexic, Bipolar, Single Parent, Diabetic, Tither, Left-brained. The labels are marginally useful for understanding some aspect of the human condition, but the moment they are used to identify a person, they obscure ... the unprecedented, unrepeatable soul addressed by God.

EUGENE H. PETERSON, *SUBVERSIVE SPIRITUALITY*

Welcome (5 Minutes)

Welcome to Session 1 of *Altar Ego*. If this is your first time together as a group, take a moment to introduce yourselves to each other before watching the video. Then let's get started!

Video: Overcoming the Labels that Bind You (12 Minutes)

Play the video segment for Session 1. As you watch, use the accompanying outline to follow along or to take notes on anything that stands out to you.

Notes

Negative labels: You are not who others say you are.

God's truth is bigger than other people's opinions about you.

An altar ego is who God says you are.

Two helpful thoughts to establish a God-centered view:

1. God can give you a new *name*.

"You will be called by a new name that the mouth of the LORD will bestow" (Isaiah 62:2).

You will grow into your new name.

2. God will give you a new *purpose*.

Simon means unpredictable, unstable, unfaithful. Jesus gave Simon the new name Peter, which means rock.

God often takes our greatest weakness and makes it our greatest strength.

It's time for you to become who God says you are.

Group Discussion (40 Minutes)

Take a few minutes to talk about what you just watched.

1. What part of the teaching had the most impact on you?

The Labeled Life

2. Briefly recall a few of the people you encountered in the last day or two — family, friends, neighbors, coworkers, restaurant or store staff, strangers you passed in your daily travels, etc.

   • What labels went through your mind as you encountered these people? Consider positive, negative, and neutral labels. For example: team player (positive), freeloader (negative), clerk (neutral).

   • What similarities and differences do you see between the labels you applied to people over the last day or two and the labels you imagine these same people may have applied to you?

   • When you think about any negative labels you may have for people you know well, what makes it especially difficult for you to let those labels go or to see the "unprecedented, unrepeatable soul" behind the label?

3. Craig described struggling with two kinds of labels: idealized, people-pleasing labels like *good son* and *good student*; and negative, confining labels like *tightwad* and *Scrooge*. He failed to live up to the idealized labels and couldn't seem to live down the negative ones.

- What labels come to mind when you think about your own struggles? For example, what idealized images have you wanted people to believe about you so you could fit in and win approval? What negative characterizations have left you feeling trapped by past behavior?

- How have these idealized or negative labels — which are largely about how others see you — impacted the way you see yourself? For example, how might they have led to self-defeating thought patterns that keep you stuck or mental labels that you use to beat yourself up?

Altar Ego

4. The alternative to a labeled life is an *altar ego*. Developing an altar ego requires sacrificing false labels in order to discover your true identity in Christ. The apostle Paul describes how this happens in his letter to the church at Colossae:

> Since you have been raised to new life with Christ, set your sights on the realities of heaven, where Christ sits in the place

of honor at God's right hand. Think about the things of heaven, not the things of earth. For you died to this life, and your real life is hidden with Christ in God (Colossians 3:1 – 3 NLT).

When Paul writes that our real life is "hidden," he uses the Greek word *krypto*. *Krypto* is the root word for several English words, including the word "encrypt," which means to encode and make secret. Encryption is a form of protection — it guards sensitive information by making it inaccessible to anyone who doesn't have the key to unlock the code.

- How does the idea of encryption help you to understand what it might mean that your real life — your true identity — is "hidden with Christ in God"?

- Why do you think God hides your true identity? From whom or from what might your true identity need to be protected?

- How would you describe the decoding "key," the means of accessing and understanding your true identity?

5. In the Bible, an *altar* is a place where people encounter God — primarily through sacrifice and worship. An *ego* is an identity — the unique collection of thoughts, feelings, traits, and behaviors that makes you *you*.

- Briefly describe your associations with altars or any personal experiences you have of altars (for example, in your church or a cathedral you visited). Are these associations and experiences mostly positive or negative, meaningful or insignificant, recent or distant, etc.?

- How have experiences of personal sacrifice — intentional decisions to surrender something important to you — shaped your identity? For example, consider time, resources, or something of yourself that you have willingly surrendered to God or offered to others. How did these willing subtractions influence your outlook, values, or decisions?

- Based on your associations with altars and your experiences of personal sacrifice, what intrigues you or concerns you about pursuing what Craig describes as an *altar ego*?

A New Name

6. An altar ego is a God-centered identity — one we both receive as a gift and grow into over time. A biblical example is the apostle Peter, whose given name was Simon. The name Simon means unpredictable, unstable, unfaithful — and it was an accurate

reflection of Simon's impulsive character. But the very first thing Jesus does when he meets Simon is rename him:

> Jesus looked at him and said, "You are Simon son of John. You will be called Cephas" (which, when translated, is Peter) (John 1:42).

Both names (Cephas is Aramaic and Peter is Greek) mean *rock*, the precise opposite of wishy-washy Simon. In essence, Jesus says, *I see you. I know who you are right now. And I know a deeper truth about who you really are.*

- Before giving Simon a new name, Jesus could easily have said, "You are *no longer* Simon." Instead, Jesus says, "You *are* Simon." How would you describe the differences in these two statements? What potential significance is there in the way Jesus chooses to make the statement?

- If Jesus were to address one of the above statements to you before giving you a new name, which one would you want him to say — *You are ...* or *You are no longer ...*? Why?

- Using John 1:42 as a reference, how would you characterize the similarities and differences between a label and an identity?

7. The four remaining sessions in *Altar Ego* take a deeper look at how we can overcome the obstacles that keep us from living out our true identity in Christ. In addition to learning together as a group, it's important to be aware of how God is at work among

you — especially in how you relate to each other and share your lives throughout the study. As you discuss the teaching in each session, there will be many opportunities to speak life-giving — and life-challenging — words, and to listen to one another deeply.

Take a few moments to consider the kinds of things that are important to you in this setting. What do you need or want from the other members of the group? Use one or more of the sentence starters below, or your own statement, to help the group understand the best way to speak life and truth to you. As each person responds, use the two-page chart that follows to briefly note what is important to that person and how you can be a good companion to them.

It really helps me when …

I tend to withdraw when …

I'll know this group is a safe place if you …

In our discussions, the best thing you could do for me is …

NAME	THE BEST WAY I CAN COMPANION THIS PERSON IS ...

NAME	THE BEST WAY I CAN COMPANION THIS PERSON IS ...

Individual Activity: What I Want to Remember (2 Minutes)

Complete this activity on your own.

1. Briefly review the outline and any notes you took.
2. In the space below, write down the most significant thing you gained in this session — from the teaching, activities, or discussions.

   What I want to remember from this session ...

Closing Prayer

Close your time together with prayer.

Personal Study

● Read and Learn

Read "To the Reader" and chapter 1 of the *Altar Ego* book. Use the space below to note any insights or questions you want to bring to the next group session.

● Study and Reflect

My ego, that self-constructed identity I worked so hard to build, came from a twisted combination of my accomplishments and other people's opinions of me.

Altar Ego, pages 8–9

1. Embracing an altar ego — the person God says we are — requires letting go of false labels that limit and obscure our true identity. Often these labels come in one of two forms: idealized labels and negative labels.

   Idealized labels represent the carefully crafted version of ourselves we work hard to create and present to the world for affirmation and approval. For example, Craig described in the group session how in high school he tried hard to present himself as successful — as a good student, a good son, a good athlete.

   Negative labels are typically a legacy of the past. They might be labels we earned through a pattern of regrettable behavior or things that other people have attached to us over the years through no fault of our own. For example, Craig described how his extreme and sometimes deceptive penny-pinching ways earned him labels like *tightwad* and *Scrooge*.

   Use the following lists to reflect on any idealized and negative labels that may have shaped your identity. In each list, check two or three labels you identify with, or write in your own label if nothing on the lists seems right.

Idealized Labels

It's important to me that other people see me as ...

☐ **Caring.** I am helpful, generous, and tuned in to others.
☐ **Successful.** I am industrious, self-motivated, and optimistic.
☐ **Unique.** I am creative, drawn to beauty, and feel things deeply.
☐ **Wise.** I am perceptive, independent, and hungry for knowledge.
☐ **Loyal.** I am supportive, reliable, and committed.
☐ **Fun.** I am spontaneous, adventurous, and joyful.
☐ **Influential.** I am strong, decisive, and protective.
☐ **Easygoing.** I am open-minded, pleasant, and accepting.
☐ **Good.** I am honest, idealistic, and self-disciplined.
☐ Other: _____

Negative Labels

I feel like I sometimes have a reputation for being ...

☐ **Prideful.** I can be manipulative, possessive, and insecure.
☐ **Deceitful.** I can be phony, competitive, and self-absorbed.
☐ **Dissatisfied.** I can be envious, self-doubting, and easily hurt.
☐ **Greedy.** I can be withdrawn, arrogant, and stingy.
☐ **Fearful.** I can be suspicious, self-defeating, and hyper-vigilant.
☐ **Self-indulgent.** I can be impulsive, self-destructive, and unfocused.
☐ **Aggressive.** I can be controlling, vindictive, and insensitive.
☐ **Lazy.** I can be apathetic, passive-aggressive, and defensive.
☐ **Angry.** I can be dogmatic, judgmental, and perfectionistic.
☐ Other: _____

Of the labels you checked, which ones would you say you struggle with most? Circle or highlight one label on each list.

What negative self-talk are you aware of in connection with these labels? For example, *I'm such a loser; I'll never be successful. No one will like me if I'm not funny. I'm worthless. I can't change.*

How do these labels and negative thought patterns tend to keep you stuck or leave you feeling disempowered?

You were made for more than you've settled for. You know your life does not reflect who you really are deep down inside.

Altar Ego, page 19

---

2. A false identity can become a safe haven of sorts. It protects us from the risk of growth and change with a lie that essentially says, *All of these labels are not only true about you, they are what is* most true *about you. They are undeniable, irreversible, and unchallengeable. This is who you are and always will be.* To get a picture of what this looks like, read the personal story Craig Groeschel shares in "The Safety of a False Identity" (see box that follows question 2). Then respond to the questions below.

Keeping in mind your responses to question 1 above, what label or issue is most likely to make you "settle" and think something like, "That's just who I am."

Craig became convinced that Amy's self-identification with being average was a lie. What potential lies do you recognize in the label you identified?

Settling for mediocrity kept Amy safe. She didn't have to work hard, risk failure, or take responsibility for developing her gifts. How do you recognize this need for safety in yourself? What is the hard work you might be avoiding, the failure you're afraid of risking, or the gifts you resist taking responsibility to develop?

The Safety of a False Identity

So often we cling to the safety of a familiar, false identity rather than extend ourselves to grasp who we really are. People tell us we're shy so we never allow ourselves to take risks to meet new people and become more social; we retreat into our safe refrain of "that's just who I am." Or they tell us we're funny and always expect us to crack a joke or deliver a witty punch line, never challenging us to use the intellect behind that humor for something more substantive.

I observed this phenomenon—and challenged it—when I first met my wife Amy over twenty-two years ago when she was a sophomore in college. Beyond her love for God, I was immediately impressed with her quick wit and sharp mind. So imagine my shock when one day Amy casually mentioned that she was just an average student. Average student? I remember thinking, *There is* nothing *average about this girl!* So I pushed back, arguing with assurance that she wasn't average at all.

Amy didn't budge on her self-proclamation of mediocrity. She dismissed my observation as the product of infatuation or misguided flattery. When I tried to discern why she felt this way about herself, she explained that everyone—her parents, her teachers, her friends—always told her she was a middle-of-the-road student. For as long as she could remember, everyone agreed that she wasn't at the bottom of the class and would never find herself at the top. Making mostly B's and a handful of C's only confirmed the only-average label.

After several more months of getting to know Amy even better, I became thoroughly convinced that she believed a lie. With a burden that I felt came from God, I sat Amy down and looked her in the eye. I told her as boldly as I could, "Just because everyone else says something and even believes it, doesn't make it true. You are not average. God made you very, very bright."

Amy's eyes almost glazed over as she instinctively brushed me off. Unfazed, I firmly but lovingly held both sides of her face and said, "Listen to me. I believe God wants you to hear this. Hear it as him speaking, not me. God did not make you average. You have greatness inside of you. It's time to act like it."

Her eyes teared and locked with mine. Something changed at that moment. Instead of seeing herself as others saw her, I believe Amy saw herself as God saw her. She started her next semester, not as Amy-the-Average, but with a new God-given name: Amy-the-Brilliant. If my story sounds a little cheesy or overly dramatic, the results speak for themselves. For the first time ever, Amy made a 4.0—all A's. With a new, God-given self-image, she never made anything lower than an A for the rest of her college studies....

What's true about you now doesn't have to be true about you later. The goal is not to reinvent yourself by striving to be some perfect person but to allow God to do an extreme makeover by uncovering your true self in his image, redeemed through Christ. What once was—no longer has to be. God can and will break the labels that have held you hostage.

Altar Ego, pages 21–23

3. An altar ego is a God-centered identity grounded in a relationship with Christ. It is your true self — no labels, no lies. Every Christ follower receives it as a gift, but it also requires something of us. Here is how Jesus explained it to his disciples:

> If any of you wants to be my follower, you must turn from your selfish ways, take up your cross, and follow me. If you try to hang on to your life, you will lose it. But if you give up your life for my sake, you will save it (Matthew 16:24 – 25 NLT).

Consider this passage again from *The Message*:

> Anyone who intends to come with me has to let me lead. You're not in the driver's seat; I am. Don't run from suffering; embrace it. Follow me and I'll show you how. Self-help is no help at all. Self-sacrifice is the way, my way, to finding yourself, your true self (Matthew 16:24 – 25 MSG).

If becoming your true self in Christ requires self-sacrifice, what might you need to let go of — either in connection to the labels you identified or in any area of your life?

How do you respond to the image of embracing this sacrifice rather than running from it? What might it mean to do this?

● Guided Prayer

God, thank you for giving me a new identity — a true identity — in you. That is the person I want to be. I know that requires letting go of some labels — idealistic ones and negative ones. A label I'm really struggling with right now is … This is hard for me because …

I also know I need to step out of the safety of my false identity and take some risks. I sense you may be challenging me to … I ask that you help me …

God, more than anything, I want to let you lead. I'm tired of trying to hang on to life just as it is. Give me the courage I need to give up my life so I can find my true self in you. Amen.

YOU ARE GOD'S MASTERPIECE

We are the work of his hands, you and I. Which is to say, we are roughly quarried stone on our way to becoming the magnum opus of God, the "great work" of his life. The work he thinks of, dreams of. The work he frets over, obsesses over. We are a masterpiece in the making. And not just any masterpiece. His masterpiece.

KEN GIRE, *SHAPED BY THE CROSS*

Group Discussion: Checking In (5 Minutes)

Welcome to Session 2 of *Altar Ego*. A key part of getting to know God better is sharing your journey with others. Before watching the video, briefly check in with each other about your experiences since the last session. For example:

- What insights did you discover in the personal study or in the chapters you read from the *Altar Ego* book?
- How did the last session impact your daily life or your relationship with God?
- What questions would you like to ask the other members of your group?

Video: You Are God's Masterpiece (10 Minutes)

Play the video segment for Session 2. As you watch, use the accompanying outline to follow along or to take notes on anything that stands out to you.

Notes

Without Christ, there is a lot wrong with us.

With Christ, we are God's masterpiece.

"God saved you by his grace when you believed. And you can't take credit for this; it is a gift from God. Salvation is not a reward for the good things we have done, so none of us can boast about it. For we are God's masterpiece. He has created us anew in Christ Jesus, so we can do the good things he planned for us long ago" (Ephesians 2:8 – 10 NLT).

We're not saved by the good works we do; we're saved by God to do good works.

Two things to think about:

1. As God's masterpiece, you were created for a purpose.

"For you created my inmost being; you knit me together in my mother's womb. I praise you because I am fearfully and wonderfully made; your works are wonderful, I know that full well. My frame was not hidden from you when I was made in the secret place, when I was woven together in the depths of the earth. Your eyes saw my unformed body; all the days ordained for me were written in your book before one of them came to be" (Psalm 139:13 – 16).

If you want to know the purpose of a thing, don't ask the thing; ask the one who created the thing.

Ask God, *What have you created me to do?*

2. You have everything you need to do everything God wants you to do.

"His divine power has given us everything we need for a godly life through our knowledge of him who called us by his own glory and goodness" (2 Peter 1:3).

The problem is, we focus on what we can't do instead of what we can do. We focus on what we are not, instead of on what we are.

Through Christ, you can be the masterpiece created for the Master's purpose.

Group Discussion (40 Minutes)

Take a few minutes to talk about what you just watched.

1. What part of the teaching had the most impact on you?

The Divine Artist

2. The biblical writers use many images for God (for example: father, judge, king, shepherd, advocate). In his letter to the church at Ephesus, the apostle Paul uses the image of God as an *artist*, a creator of beauty in human beings:

> For we are God's *masterpiece*. He has created us anew in Christ Jesus, so we can do the good things he planned for us long ago (Ephesians 2:10 NLT, emphasis added).

- What comes to mind when you imagine God as an artist? In contrast with other biblical images, how does this image reveal something unique about who God is and how God works?

- In what ways, if any, would you say you have recently experienced God as an artist — someone who works to create goodness and beauty in you?

3. The Greek word translated in the Ephesians passage as "masterpiece" is the noun *poiema* (poy´-ay-mah). In literal translation it means "what is made, work, creation."[1] A Greek translation of the Old Testament called the Septuagint often uses the verb form of *poiema* (*poieo*) to describe God's creative activity in the world:

> Who among the gods is like you, LORD? Who is like you — majestic in holiness, awesome in glory, *working* wonders? (Exodus 15:11, emphasis added)

> Praise be to the LORD God, the God of Israel, who alone *does* marvelous deeds (Psalm 72:18, emphasis added).

---

1. Friedrich Thiele, "*poiema*," *New International Dictionary of New Testament Theology*, vol. 3, Colin Brown, gen. ed. (Grand Rapids: Zondervan, 1978, 1986), 1152.

This is the day the LORD has *made*. We will rejoice and be glad in it (Psalm 118:24 NLT, emphasis added).

He *performs* wonders that cannot be fathomed, miracles that cannot be counted (Job 5:9, emphasis added).

In these verses, God's work is "masterpiecing." He master-pieces everything he creates — from an ordinary day to marvel-ous deeds, unfathomable wonders, and countless miracles.

- Consider an experience of masterpiecing in your own life — a project or event that was important to you and to which you devoted an extraordinary amount of time, resources, and effort. It could be anything — creating an art project, writing music, restoring a vintage car, planning a wedding, etc. Briefly describe the impact this project had on you during the process. For example, how did it change what you thought about, how you felt, how you spent your time, how you related to others, etc. What kind of thoughts or feelings did you have about the project itself?

- What insights does your experience of working on this project or event provide about God's masterpiecing work in human beings — how he "creates us anew in Christ Jesus"?

Created for a Purpose

4. Without Christ, Scripture confirms that we are not only lost but without purpose:

   All have turned away; all have become useless. No one does good, not a single one (Romans 3:12 NLT).

With Christ, we share a common purpose: to love God and love others (Matthew 22:37 – 40) by doing "the good things [God] planned for us long ago" (Ephesians 2:10 NLT). God also gives each of us a distinct purpose — specific gifts enabling us to fulfill God's unique call on our lives (Romans 12:6).

Which of the statements below comes closest to your current perspective about your gifts and purpose? Share the reasons for your response.

☐ I am clear about my gifts and actively engaged in living out my purpose.

☐ I have a good idea about my gifts and am taking steps to live out my purpose more fully.

☐ I am somewhat uncertain about my gifts and my purpose seems to change during different seasons of my life. Sometimes I feel like I am living out my purpose and other times I wonder if I've missed it.

☐ I am in a process of discovery. I am trying to figure out what my gifts are and how to live out my purpose.

☐ I am unclear about my gifts and I struggle when it comes to knowing my purpose and living it out.

☐ Other: _____

5. Following are five verses that shed light on what it means to live with purpose. Go around the group and have a different person read each passage aloud. As the passages are read, underline or highlight any words or phrases that stand out to you. You may wish to read through the list twice to give everyone time to listen and respond.

> If you keep growing in this way, it will show that what you know about our Lord Jesus Christ has made your lives useful and meaningful (2 Peter 1:8 CEV).

God chose you, and we keep praying that God will make you worthy of being his people. We pray for God's power to help you do all the good things that you hope to do and that your faith makes you want to do (2 Thessalonians 1:11 CEV).

This is to my Father's glory, that you bear much fruit, showing yourselves to be my disciples (John 15:8).

Always work enthusiastically for the Lord, for you know that nothing you do for the Lord is ever useless (1 Corinthians 15:58 NLT).

Whatever you do, do it all for the glory of God (1 Corinthians 10:31).

- Which of the five verses stands out most to you? Why?

- The verse from 2 Peter affirms lives that are "useful and meaningful." In what area of your life right now do you have the strongest sense of feeling useful and meaningful? What connections, if any, do you make between this area of your life and your unique gifts and purpose? (If you struggle to identify an area of life in which you have a strong sense of feeling useful and meaningful, describe the area of life in which you sense the greatest need to feel useful and meaningful. How do you hope God might work in you to change this area of your life?)

Everything You Need

6. Even when we're uncertain about our unique gifts and purpose, Scripture affirms that God has already provided everything we need to live for him:

God is able to bless you abundantly, so that in all things at all times, having all that you need, you will abound in every good work (2 Corinthians 9:8).

We have everything we need to live a life that pleases God. It was all given to us by God's own power, when we learned that he had invited us to share in his wonderful goodness. God made great and marvelous promises, so that his nature would become part of us (2 Peter 1:3 – 4a CEV).

- Which number on the continuum below best describes your perspective? Share the reasons for your response.

1	2	3	4	5	6	7	8	9	10

I feel like I am missing something or that my circumstances need to be different in order to live my best life for God.

No matter what my circumstances are, I feel like I have everything I need to live my best life for God.

- Briefly identify an area of life (for example: a difficult relationship, a complex problem, a temptation or sin pattern, an urgent need, an emotional wound, etc.) in which you are most aware of feeling like you don't have what you need to live a life that pleases God. Overall, how do the passages from 2 Corinthians and 2 Peter impact how you feel about this issue? Do they encourage you or discourage you? Why?

7. At the end of the group discussion for Session 1, you had the opportunity to share what you need from the other members of the group, and to write down the best ways you can be good companions to one another.

- Briefly restate what you asked for from the group in Session 1. What changes or clarifications would you like to make that would help the group know more about how to be a good companion to you? As each person responds, add any additional information to the Session 1 chart. (If you were absent from the last session, share your response to Session 1 question 7. Then use the chart to write down what is important to each member of the group.)

- In what ways, if any, did you find yourself responding differently to other members of the group in this session based on what they asked for in the previous session? What made that easy or difficult for you to do?

Individual Activity: What I Want to Remember (2 Minutes)

1. Briefly review the outline and any notes you took.
2. In the space below, write down the most significant thing you gained in this session — from the teaching, activities, or discussions.

What I want to remember from this session ...

Closing Prayer

Close your time together with prayer.

Personal Study

● Read and Learn

Read chapters 2 – 4 of the *Altar Ego* book. Use the space below to note any insights or questions you want to bring to the next group session.

● Study and Reflect

By ourselves, we'll never be enough. But once we surrender our lives to God, everything about us—including our mistakes and weaknesses—becomes the raw material for his masterpiece.

Altar Ego, page 34

1. Every good creation begins as raw material. No matter how messed up our lives may be when we surrender ourselves to God, he uses all the material we give him to remake us into something whole and beautiful:

   For we are God's masterpiece. He has created us anew in Christ Jesus, so we can do the good things he planned for us long ago (Ephesians 2:10 NLT).

   For a fresh perspective on this familiar verse, consider it again in these alternate versions:

   For we are his workmanship, created in Christ Jesus for good works, which God prepared beforehand, that we should walk in them (ESV).

   We are his design; God has created us in Christ Jesus, pledged to such good actions as he has prepared beforehand, to be the employment of our lives (KNOX).

   [God] creates each of us by Christ Jesus to join him in the work he does, the good work he has gotten ready for us to do, work we had better be doing (MSG).

The Greek verb translated as "created/creates" is *ktizō* (ktid´-zo). It is used by New Testament writers to describe creative work that only God can do (see for example Mark 13:9; Ephesians 3:9; Colossians 1:16, 3:10). More specifically, it means to "make or create something which has not existed before."[2]

What comes to mind when you reflect on the work that God has already done in your life? For example, what is it that is true about your identity or your life that did not exist before you gave your life to Christ?

Where are you most aware of a need for God to do something completely new in you now?

The purpose of God's creative work is that we "walk" in the good work he has prepared for us. The Greek verb the ESV translates as "walk in" is *peripateō* (per-ee-pat-eh´-o), and it is used here to describe not just actions but a way of life — one that stands in stark contrast to the "trespasses and sins in which you once *walked*," which is our old way of life (Ephesians 2:1 ESV, emphasis added). It is this lifestyle of walking-around goodness that is our lifelong "employment."

---

2. J. P. Louw and Eugene Albert Nida, "Make, Create," 42.35, *Greek-English Lexicon of the New Testament*, Second Edition (New York: United Bible Societies, 1988, 1989), 514.

Briefly reflect on your activities and relationships over the last twenty-four hours. To what degree would you say your behaviors and interactions were characterized by walking-around goodness? Circle the number on the continuum that best describes your response.

| 1 | 2 | 3 | 4 | 5 | 6 | 7 | 8 | 9 | 10 |

My behaviors and interactions were characterized primarily by my old way of life.

My behaviors and interactions were characterized primarily by my new way of life.

If you could do the day over again, what would you change? For example, what would you do more of (and what would you do less of) to reflect more of God's goodness in your behaviors and interactions?

God decided that ... this was the single point ideally suited for you to serve him and bring him glory. Out of all the nearly infinite possibilities, there was no better time for you to be born with your unique gifts, talents, skills, and personality. God knew you before you were, and he put you right where he wanted you.

Altar Ego, pages 37–38

2. God saves us so we can make a difference and bring glory to him. Consider these two compelling statements Jesus makes that reveal something about what it means to bring glory to God:

"This is to my Father's glory, that you bear much fruit, showing yourselves to be my disciples" (John 15:8).

"[Father,] I have brought you glory on earth by finishing the work you gave me to do" (John 17:4).

Briefly consider the things that are difficult or unknowns for you right now. If everything about those circumstances were to remain unchanged for the foreseeable future, how would it impact your understanding of what it means to bring glory to God in your life right now? How do you imagine it might diminish or increase your ability to bear much fruit and do the work God has given you to do right where you are?

Bringing glory to God is not about gritty self-effort, trying really hard to be good, or merely keeping busy with good activities; it's about joining God in the work he is already doing — especially the work he is doing in us:

Now all glory to God, who is able, through his mighty power at work within us, to accomplish infinitely more than we might ask or think (Ephesians 3:20 NLT).

For God is working in you, giving you the desire and the power to do what pleases him (Philippians 2:13 NLT).

What is the "more than" you hope God might do *in* you? How do you hope it might enable God to do more *through* you?

In what circumstance, decision, or relationship are you most aware of needing a greater desire or more power to do what pleases God?

Believing that you are precisely where God wants you to be right now, what is something only you could do to bring God glory within the next twenty-four hours?

● Guided Prayer

God, thank you for your creative work in my life, for taking what is hard and broken about me and shaping it into a masterpiece.

I know I will always be a work in process — I still have hard and broken pieces that need the creative work that only you can do. Please create something new in me, specifically in connection with ... I need your help because ...

I know that you want me to be fruitful, but I'm not always certain if I'm doing the work you've given me to do, both now and in the future. Right now, I ask for guidance about ... For the future, I ask for guidance about ...

Lord, I know that every day is full of opportunities for walking-around goodness. Every day I can be fruitful in loving and serving the people you bring into my life. Please give me a greater desire and more power to do what pleases you so that I can complete the work you have given me to do. Amen.

TRADING THE IMMEDIATE FOR THE ULTIMATE

The important thing is this: To be able at any moment to sacrifice what we are for what we could become.

CHARLES DU BOS, *APPROXIMATIONS*

Group Discussion: Checking In (5 Minutes)

Welcome to Session 3 of *Altar Ego*. A key part of getting to know God better is sharing your journey with others. Before watching the video, briefly check in with each other about your experiences since the last session. For example:

- What insights did you discover in the personal study or in the chapters you read from the *Altar Ego* book?
- How did the last session impact your daily life or your relationship with God?
- What questions would you like to ask the other members of your group?

Video: Trading the Immediate for the Ultimate (11 Minutes)

Play the video segment for Session 3. As you watch, use the accompanying outline to follow along or to take notes on anything that stands out to you.

Notes

Throughout biblical history, people give in to their fleshly desires: *I deserve this. I need to get what I want. If it feels good, do it.*

"For the world offers only a craving for physical pleasure, a craving for everything we see, and pride in our achievements and possessions. These are not from the Father, but are from this world. And this world is fading away, along with everything that people crave. But anyone who does what pleases God will live forever" (1 John 2:16 – 17 NLT).

Two big problems when people have an entitled ego:

1. They want what they want now, not later.

    Example: the prodigal son (Luke 15)

2. They are willing to trade the ultimate for the immediate.

    Example: Jacob and Esau (Genesis 25)

    People do this every day; they let their immediate desires overcome the longer-term benefit.

Learn to do two things:

1. Trade the immediate for the ultimate.

    "Better to be patient than powerful; better to have self-control than to conquer a city" (Proverbs 16:32 NLT).

When you know who you are, you'll sacrifice what you want, to become who God really wants you to be.

You'll often overestimate what you can accomplish in the short run, but you'll almost always underestimate what you can accomplish in the long run.

2. Seek God until his desires become your desires.

"Take delight in the LORD, and he will give you the desires of your heart" (Psalm 37:4).

Group Discussion (40 Minutes)

Take a few minutes to talk about what you just watched.

1. What part of the teaching had the most impact on you?

The Cookie Game

2. Craig described how he teaches his kids the benefits of delayed gratification by offering them a choice: one cookie now or three cookies if they wait an hour.

Thinking back to what you can recall about yourself as a young child, how do you imagine your five-year-old self might have responded to the cookie game? As an adult, would you say your tendency has changed or mostly stayed the same?

3. Which statement below best describes your typical thought process when you do choose immediate gratification? If you can think of any, share an experience from the last day or two that illustrates your response.

☐ **I prioritize:** This is important. I want this more than anything else right now.

☐ **I rationalize:** What I want is so reasonable and normal, it would be practically unreasonable and abnormal not to have it.

☐ **I romanticize:** If I have this, I will feel happy and complete.

☐ **I globalize:** Everyone else has this, so I should have it too.

☐ **I exceptionalize:** I know I shouldn't have this, but these are special circumstances.

☐ **I "justifize":** I've had a hard day/week/life. I deserve this.

☐ Other: _____

The Entitled Ego

4. When we are operating out of an entitled ego, we allow our feelings to become reasons that justify our desires; and our desires demand satisfaction — now. Here is how the apostle John describes this kind of mindset:

> For the world offers only a craving for physical pleasure, a craving for everything we see, and pride in our achievements and possessions. These are not from the Father, but are from this

world. And this world is fading away, along with everything that people crave. But anyone who does what pleases God will live forever (1 John 2:16 – 17 NLT).

In his letter to the church at Galatia, the apostle Paul contrasts this entitled ego mindset with what we might call the altar ego mindset:

So I say, let the Holy Spirit guide your lives. Then you won't be doing what your sinful nature craves. The sinful nature wants to do evil, which is just the opposite of what the Spirit wants. And the Spirit gives us desires that are the opposite of what the sinful nature desires. These two forces are constantly fighting each other, so you are not free to carry out your good intentions (Galatians 5:16 – 17 NLT).

- The passages make a distinction between entitled ego desires (that come from the world) and altar ego desires (that come from the Spirit). Overall, to what degree would you say you are aware of the source of your desires — as coming from the sinful nature or the Spirit — when you have to make a choice about something you want? For example, are you very aware, somewhat aware, or unaware? How does your level of awareness tend to impact your choice?

- The Galatians passage describes the two kinds of desires as "forces that are constantly fighting each other." Briefly identify an area of life and an issue in which you experience this kind of battle between your desires. For example, it might be an issue related to your finances, health, or relationships. If you were to characterize your choice as trading the ultimate for the immediate, what would you say is the *ultimate*, and what is the *immediate*?

- In the moment, what is it about your *immediate* that makes it seem worth the trade? What are you afraid of missing out on, or how does the thought of not having what you want impact you?

5. Choosing the ultimate over the immediate requires exercising self-control. The author of Proverbs writes:

> Better to be patient than powerful; better to have self-control than to conquer a city (Proverbs 16:32 NLT).

> Losing self-control leaves you as helpless as a city without a wall (Proverbs 25:28 CEV).

On the video, Craig noted characters from the Bible who paid a high price when they failed to exercise self-control: Eve chose the forbidden fruit; David chose adultery; Moses chose murder; Esau chose a bowl of stew.

- In each of these stories, how do you recognize the dynamics of power and helplessness the Proverbs writer describes? In other words, how did what initially seemed like an exercise of power ultimately render each person helpless?

- In the moment when you are tempted with a choice between an immediate and an ultimate, which option makes you feel more powerful? Why?

Take Delight

6. In the Galatians 5 passage, Paul says that the Spirit gives us desires. It is a truth the psalmist already knew well:

> Take delight in the LORD, and he will give you the desires of your heart (Psalm 37:4).

The psalmist proposes a win-win exchange — delight for desires. The verb translated "delight" is the Hebrew word *anag* (aw-nag´). It conveys the idea of indulgence, being pampered, and taking great pleasure in something. The invitation is to luxuriate in the Lord, to discover that "true self-fulfillment does not lie in a preoccupation with self but in selfless preoccupation with God."[3]

- Briefly describe an experience of delighting in another person — a time when you were utterly captivated and wanted nothing more than to be with him or her. For example: holding a newborn, playing with a young child, falling in love, talking with someone who thoroughly fascinated you.

- Using your experience as a reference, how would you describe what it means to delight in the Lord?

7. Take a few moments to reflect on what you've learned and experienced together in this study so far.

- How has learning more about developing an altar ego impacted you?

---

3. Douglas Carew, "'ng," *New International Dictionary of Old Testament Theology and Exegesis*, vol. 3, Willem A. VanGemeren, gen. ed. (Grand Rapids: Zondervan, 1997), 443 – 444.

- Since the first session, what shifts have you noticed in yourself in terms of how you relate to the group? For example, do you feel more or less guarded, understood, challenged, encouraged, connected, etc.?

- What adjustments, if any, would you like to make to the Session 1 chart that would help other members of the group know how to be better companions for you?

Individual Activity: **What I Want to Remember** (2 Minutes)

1. Briefly review the outline and any notes you took.
2. In the space below, write down the most significant thing you gained in this session — from the teaching, activities, or discussions.

   What I want to remember from this session …

Closing Prayer

Close your time together with prayer.

Personal Study

● Read and Learn

Read chapter 5 of the *Altar Ego* book. Use the space below to note any insights or questions you want to bring to the next group session.

● Study and Reflect

What have [we] done to ourselves? We've traded the ultimate (God's blessings) for the immediate (our selfish desires). We've given away our birthright for a stupid bowl of stew.

Altar Ego, page 93

---

1. One of the most vivid examples of trading the ultimate for the immediate is the Old Testament story of Esau. As the eldest of two brothers, Esau's rights as the firstborn — his birthright — gave him significant advantages over Jacob. These included a paternal blessing, leadership and authority over the extended family, twice the inheritance, and special status with God as heir to the covenant promise given to Abraham. In material terms, it might be something like a multi-million-dollar trust fund, title to the family's extensive real estate holdings, and a majority stake in the family business. But in a weak moment, Esau trades it all for the equivalent of a burger and fries.

    Read Esau's story in Genesis 25:29 – 34.

    Compare and contrast the condition of both brothers at the beginning of the story. What does the text reveal about their *immediate* — what each one wants most in the moment?

The *ultimate* at stake for both brothers is the birthright — a future blessing based on God's promise to Abraham. How would you characterize each brother's approach to the birthright and their level of belief in the promise?

The fulfillment of any promise requires waiting. Why do you imagine that Jacob was able to wait but Esau was not?

You might ask, "Who in the world would do something as stupid as trade their birthright for a bowl of stew?" If you think about it, you already know the answer. We do it every single day.

Altar Ego, page 91

2. We all have our Esau moments, times we face a choice between what we want in the moment and the greater thing we could have if we wait. Using the chart that follows, briefly identify some of the issues you face that tempt you to choose the immediate over the ultimate.

AREA OF LIFE	THE IMMEDIATE What I Could Have Right Away	THE ULTIMATE What I Could Have If I Wait
Personal Finances earning, giving, saving, spending, debt		
Physical Health food, exercise, rest, medical care		
Relationships loving words and actions with family, friends, colleagues, neighbors		
Spiritual Life putting God first, regular practice of spiritual disciplines (prayer, study, time alone with God, journaling, etc.)		
Pace of Life sustainability, stewardship of daily time, over- or under-scheduling		
Marriage, Dating, Sexuality intimacy, connection, affirmation, commitment, integrity		

What stands out most to you about what you wrote in the Immediate column? What connections, if any, do you make between Esau's behavior in the Genesis passage and your experience of choosing the immediate?

Reflect on the promises represented by what you wrote in the Ultimate column. In what ways, if any, do you tend to diminish or disregard the significance of these promises just as Esau "despised" his birthright?

Living with patience is better than muscling forward to demand what you want before the time is right. Self-control often unlocks the door to longer lasting, more meaningful blessings. Patience comes from knowing you already have enough of what you need the most.

Altar Ego, page 100

---

3. It's nearly impossible to wait — to say no to the demands of an entitled ego — under our own power. But the promise of Scripture is, we don't have to do it on our own:

> By his divine power, God has given us everything we need for living a godly life. We have received all of this by coming to know him, the one who called us to himself by means of his

marvelous glory and excellence. And because of his glory and excellence, he has given us great and precious promises. These are the promises that enable you to share his divine nature and escape the world's corruption caused by human desires. In view of all this, make every effort to respond to God's promises (2 Peter 1:3 – 5a NLT).

When we commit our lives to Christ and enter into a relationship with him, we get immediate access to everything we need to live for God. And it's wrapped up in an ultimate promise — that the more we come to know Christ, the more like Christ we will become.

What *immediate* versus *ultimate* temptation would you say is the most difficult for you right now?

When the entitled ego is in charge, we insist on taking, defending, managing, and controlling what we desire. We must have our own way; we must meet our own needs on our own terms in our own timing.

How do you recognize these dynamics in yourself and the challenge you identified?

When the altar ego is in charge, we are content to wait and to sacrifice. We cooperate with God, affirming our trust in his promises. We receive everything God gives as a gift, allowing him to meet our needs on his terms and in his timing.

What do you sense God's loving invitation to you might be in connection with the challenge you identified?

● Guided Prayer

God, thank you for being my ultimate — the merciful God who loves me and wants to give me only good things. I confess that in my day-to-day life, I do still have my Esau moments when I am tempted to settle for so much less. An "immediate" that is especially hard for me right now is … I find it difficult to resist because …

I claim your promises that I share in your divine nature and that you have already given me everything I need to live for you. Help me to wait for you in regard to … This is an "ultimate" that means a lot to me because …

Lord, I ask for contentment and self-control. I don't want my entitled ego to be in charge; I want you to be in charge. Give me a heart that beats with your desires, an altar ego that lives for you. That is what I want more than anything. Amen.

LIVING WITH INTEGRITY

Hypocrisy is a slow-growing cancer. It's a lazy replacement of an interior that chases after God with an exterior that only seems to. No one ever sets out to be a hypocrite, but many end up there.

EUGENE H. PETERSON, *TELL IT SLANT*

Group Discussion: Checking In (5 Minutes)

Welcome to Session 4 of *Altar Ego*. A key part of getting to know God better is sharing your journey with others. Before watching the video, briefly check in with each other about your experiences since the last session. For example:

- What insights did you discover in the personal study or in the chapters you read from the *Altar Ego* book?
- How did the last session impact your daily life or your relationship with God?
- What questions would you like to ask the other members of your group?

Video: Living with Integrity (10 Minutes)

Play the video segment for Session 4. As you watch, use the accompanying outline to follow along or to take notes on anything that stands out to you.

Notes

We live in a world where lack of integrity is the norm.

Integrity is when your behavior matches your beliefs. It's who you are when no one is looking.

Example: The prophet Samuel

Four benefits of integrity:

1. You can walk closely with God.

2. You have a built-in guide (divine GPS).

3. You'll have constant peace.

4. You build trust, honor, respect, and influence.

The opposite of integrity is hypocrisy.

The big question: What is your integrity worth?

If you don't have integrity, you don't have anything; but if you have integrity, you have everything that matters.

Group Discussion (40 Minutes)

Take a few minutes to talk about what you just watched.

1. What part of the teaching had the most impact on you?

Shocking Integrity

2. Craig told a story about a cashier who was shocked — and grateful — when he did the right thing by returning the extra change she had given him by mistake.

   Briefly describe a recent experience of integrity that surprised you or someone you know. What was the expected response that made doing the right thing so surprising?

3. Craig also shared a story about honoring a promise to give his expensive tennis racket to a young student who beat him in a match. In the case of the cashier, his small act of integrity had a big and immediate impact (she got to keep her job). In the case of the tennis racket, the impact was ultimately even bigger (a man committing his life to Christ), but Craig didn't know about it until many years later.

   - To what degree would you say that your decisions about whether or not to do the right thing are influenced by how much impact you think your actions will have? In other words, if you think it won't have much of an impact, you might let it slide; if you think it will have an impact, you're more likely to do the right thing.

- How do these stories of immediate and delayed impact challenge or encourage you about something in your life right now? What relationship, situation, or decision comes to mind?

Integrity versus Hypocrisy

4. Integrity is a significant concern addressed by the apostle Paul in his second letter to the church at Corinth. His integrity is at stake because an element in the church has questioned his motives and challenged his authority as an apostle. In defending himself and his companion Timothy, Paul writes:

> Our conscience testifies that we have conducted ourselves in the world, and especially in our relations with you, with *integrity* and godly *sincerity*. We have done so, relying not on worldly wisdom but on God's grace (2 Corinthians 1:12, emphasis added).

The Greek word translated here as "integrity" is *haplotēs* (haplot´-ace). Its root is a compound of the words *ha* (together) and *pel* (to fold), meaning single or singleness. When used by Paul and other New Testament writers, it suggests "personal wholeness, undividedness … uncomplicated simplicity …. oneness of heart."[4] It can also be translated as "holiness." Paul provides both emphasis and a compelling image when he follows up with the word "sincerity," which is the Greek word *eilikrineia* (i-lik-ree´-ni-ah). *Eilikrineia* refers to something "examined by the light of the sun and found pure."[5]

---

4. Burkhard Gartner, "*haplotēs,*" *New International Dictionary of New Testament Theology*, vol. 3, Colin Brown, gen. ed. (Grand Rapids: Zondervan, 1978, 1986), 572.
5. R. H. Strachan, *The Second Epistle of Paul to the Corinthians*, Moffatt New Testament Commentary (London: Hodder and Stoughton, 1935), 54. Quoted in David E. Garland, *The New American Commentary, 2 Corinthians*, vol. 29 (Nashville: Broadman and Holman, 1999), 90.

- Which of the images or words used to define the two Greek words stands out most to you? How does it inform your understanding of what it means to have integrity?

- Paul notes that integrity and sincerity characterize both his conduct and his relationships. Do you think it's possible to make a distinction between the two — to have integrity in one area but not the other? Why or why not?

- Paul also notes that integrity and sincerity characterize his work in both the world and in the church. What demands does each context place on your integrity and sincerity? In other words, how is your integrity uniquely challenged within the Christian community? And how is it uniquely challenged in the world?

5. The opposite of integrity is hypocrisy, a condition Jesus repeatedly condemned, especially in religious leaders of the day.

> Jesus turned first to his disciples and warned them, "Beware of the yeast of the Pharisees — their *hypocrisy*. The time is coming when everything that is covered up will be revealed, and all that is secret will be made known to all. Whatever you have said in the dark will be heard in the light, and what you have whispered behind closed doors will be shouted from the housetops for all to hear!" (Luke 12:1b – 3 NLT, emphasis added).

The Greek and English words for "hypocrisy" are virtually identical. In ancient Greece, *hypokrisis* (hoop-ok´-ree-sis) referred to the action of a stage actor — called a *hypokritēs* (hoop-ok-ree-tace´) — who wore a mask to play a role. New Testament writers use *hypokrisis* to describe "behavior that attempts to cover up sin by putting oneself in a favorable light at the expense of truth."[6]

In warning his disciples against hypocrisy, Jesus uses a series of contrasts. For example, he contrasts "covered up" with "revealed." Use the following chart to briefly identify all the contrasts in the passage.

HYPOCRISY	THE OPPOSITE OF HYPOCRISY
Example: covered up	*Example:* revealed

6. Walther Günther, "*hypokrisis, hypokritēs*" *New International Dictionary of New Testament Theology*, vol. 2, Colin Brown, gen. ed. (Grand Rapids: Zondervan, 1978, 1986), 468–69.

- What stands out most to you about the two lists of words on the chart? What additional clarity do the lists provide about what it means to have integrity?

- Note Jesus' use of the words *whatever* and *everything*, as well as his repeated use of the word *all*. How does Jesus' use of these words inform your understanding about the relative impact of an integrity decision (discussed in question 3)?

- One theologian describes the hypocrisy Jesus condemns in religious leaders as a "self-deluding blindness."[7] In other words, they start out trying to deceive others but end up deceiving only themselves. How do you recognize this dynamic in yourself? In other words, how might your attempts at image management — sacrificing truth to put yourself in a more favorable light — ultimately prevent you from seeing the true state of your heart?

The Worth of Integrity

6. Craig's high school tennis coach said to him, "If you'll steal a golf ball, you'll steal something bigger — you'll lie, you'll compromise, you'll cheat." The coach was essentially saying, *If you'll trade your integrity for the price of a golf ball, you'll trade it for anything.*

---

7. Walther Günther, *New International Dictionary of New Testament Theology*, 470.

- The coach's zero tolerance policy and direct confrontation had a lasting impact on Craig. Has anyone ever challenged you about an integrity lapse? If so, how did you respond? If not, can you recall a time you wish someone had challenged you?

- If someone within this group were to challenge you about an integrity lapse, how would you want the person to do it? What would make you most receptive to what he or she had to say?

7. Take a moment to touch base with each other about how you're doing in the group. Use one of the sentence starters below, or your own statement, to help the group learn more about how to be good companions to you.

   I want to give you permission to challenge me more about ...

   An area where I really need your help or sensitivity is ...

   It always helps me to feel more connected to the group when ...

   Something I've learned about myself because of this group is ...

Individual Activity: What I Want to Remember (2 Minutes)

1. Briefly review the outline and any notes you took.

2. In the space below, write down the most significant thing you gained in this session — from the teaching, activities, or discussions.

What I want to remember from this session ...

Closing Prayer

Close your time together with prayer.

GET A HEAD START ON THE DISCUSSION FOR SESSION 5

As part of the group discussion for Session 5, you'll have an opportunity to talk about what you've learned and experienced together throughout the *Altar Ego* study. Between now and your next meeting, consider taking a few moments to review the previous sessions and identify the teaching, discussions, or activities that stand out most to you. Use the following worksheet to briefly summarize the highlights of what you've learned and experienced.

Session 5 Head Start Worksheet

Take a few moments to reflect on what you've learned and experienced throughout the *Altar Ego* study. You may want to review notes from the video teaching, what you wrote down for "What I Want to Remember" at the end of each group session, responses in the personal studies, etc. Here are some questions you might consider as part of your review:

- What insights did I gain from this session?
- What was the most important thing I learned about myself in this session?
- How did I experience God's presence or leading related to this session?
- How did this session impact my relationships with the other people in the group?

Use the spaces provided to briefly summarize what you've learned and experienced for each session.

Session 1: Overcoming the Labels that Bind You

Session 2: You Are God's Masterpiece

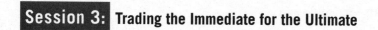

Session 3: Trading the Immediate for the Ultimate

Session 4: Living with Integrity

Personal Study

● Read and Learn

Read chapters 6 – 8 of the *Altar Ego* book. Use the space below to note any insights or questions you want to bring to the next group session.

● Study and Reflect

It doesn't make any difference if people appear to be righteous. What matters is to be pure on the inside.

Altar Ego, page 111

---

1. Practicing integrity requires that behavior match beliefs. The challenge, perhaps especially for people of faith, is that it is possible to *do* everything right and still not *be* right. This was the kind of hypocrisy Jesus ruthlessly condemned in the religious leaders of his day:

    "What sorrow awaits you teachers of religious law and you Pharisees. Hypocrites! For you are so careful to clean the outside of the cup and the dish, but inside you are filthy — full of greed and self-indulgence! You blind Pharisee! First wash the inside of the cup and the dish, and then the outside will become clean, too" (Matthew 23:25 – 26 NLT).

    If every integrity compromise is for a perceived benefit, how would you describe the benefit(s) the Pharisees got from focusing on right *doing* at the expense of right *being*?

How do you recognize this tendency to focus on right doing at the expense of right being within yourself and others in your faith community? For example, a person displays a meticulous commitment to tithing but is stingy with grace or forgiveness.

What is the perceived benefit you or others in your faith community experience, and how does it compare with the benefit(s) you identified for the Pharisees?

Through Christ, we clean the inside of the cup before we move on to the outside. We sacrifice our selfish, deceitful, ego-driven impulses on the altar of truth so that our behavior reflects God's righteousness. Integrity starts from the inside out, not the outside in.

Altar Ego, page 111

---

2. Integrity is an inside job — it begins with the heart. The group study for this session defined the Greek word for "integrity," *haplotēs* (hap-lot´-ace), as "personal wholeness, undividedness … oneness of heart." It's the kind of heart God promises to give us when we surrender ourselves to him:

And I will give them singleness of heart and put a new spirit within them. I will take away their stony, stubborn heart and give them a tender, responsive heart, so they will obey my decrees and regulations. Then they will truly be my people, and I will be their God (Ezekiel 11:19 – 20 NLT).

In what two or three areas of your life are you most aware of feeling split — that your beliefs and behaviors are consistently at odds?

In what ways, if any, would you say these splits have made your heart stony or stubborn toward God? For example, consider where you are resistant to obedience, unwilling to let go, willfully blind to the state of your heart, etc.

What, if anything, are you afraid might be required of you if God were to give you a tender, responsive heart?

If you could experience an undividedness or oneness of heart, what changes would you hope to experience — in your life and in your relationship with God?

To become a true person of integrity, the first thing you have to do is get to know Jesus ... you can never live a life of integrity on your own.

Altar Ego, page 118

3. Scripture's promise to a surrendered heart is that God is always at work in you, "giving you the *desire* and the *power* to do what pleases him" (Philippians 2:13 NLT, emphasis added).

   Keeping in mind your responses to question 2, where are you most aware of needing a stronger desire for God and more power to please God?

● Guided Prayer

God, thank you for loving me with an undivided heart, and for treating me with integrity. I know you will always keep your promises to me.

I ask that you help me to live with integrity. Sometimes I feel like I'm more concerned with looking good on the outside than I am with being good on the inside. Other times, I don't even try to match up my behaviors with my beliefs, and I really am a hypocrite. I need your help most with ... because ...

I know that integrity is an inside job, and that I need an undivided heart. I believe you can heal the split I feel inside. Please make me tender and responsive to you, especially in connection with ... As much as I want a new heart, I'm also afraid of what it might require of me ...

God, to the degree that I am able, I surrender my heart to you. I claim the promise that you are always at work in me and that you will give me the power and the desire to live for you — this day and every day. Amen.

DEVELOPING SPIRITUAL BOLDNESS

Therefore, since we have such a hope, we are very bold.

2 Corinthians 3:12

Group Discussion: Checking In (5 Minutes)

Welcome to Session 5 of *Altar Ego*. A key part of getting to know God better is sharing your journey with others. Before watching the video, briefly check in with each other about your experiences since the last session. For example:

- What insights did you discover in the personal study or in the chapters you read from the *Altar Ego* book?
- How did the last session impact your daily life or your relationship with God?
- What questions would you like to ask the other members of your group?

Video: Developing Spiritual Boldness (12 Minutes)

Play the video segment for Session 5. As you watch, use the accompanying outline to follow along or to take notes on anything that stands out to you.

Notes

Boldness is behavior born out of belief that God is who he says he is.

Example: Peter

- He had bold intentions but he failed Jesus.

- He had a change of beliefs, and boldness was born out of that belief.

- When Peter preached, 3,000 people were saved.

- He challenged religious leaders who had the power to take his life (Acts 4:8 – 9).

God specializes in giving ordinary people extraordinary boldness.

The key to developing spiritual boldness is to spend time with Jesus.

The goal is not to be bold; the goal is to know Jesus.

Boldness is a byproduct of knowing Jesus. The opposite is true as well.

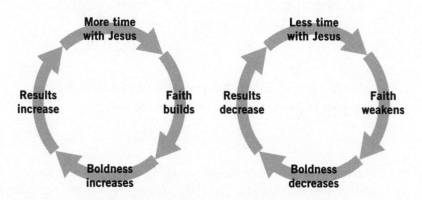

When you lay down your life and sacrifice who you are, you can become who God wants you to be.

Group Discussion (40 Minutes)

Take a few minutes to talk about what you just watched.

1. What part of the teaching had the most impact on you?

Risky Boldness

2. Boldness is behavior born out of the belief that God is who he says he is. This belief gives us confidence to take risks. People who are bold for God know when to push beyond the normal rules of politeness and willingly risk things like embarrassment, rejection, or even retaliation to speak about their faith.

   - Briefly describe an act of spiritual boldness you've witnessed, recently or in the past. (If you can't think of one, reference the example Craig shared of giving his testimony at the college athletic banquet.)

   - What did the bold person risk by speaking out? If you had been in this person's shoes, do you think you would have taken the same risk? Why or why not?

   - How did people respond to what the bold person said? How did your response resemble or differ from theirs?

   - Overall, how did witnessing this act of boldness impact you? For example, did it encourage or discourage you from taking a similar risk yourself?

3. The early church was in a risky situation. The same religious leaders who opposed Jesus and conspired to have him killed were just as intent on suppressing his followers. After Peter and John healed a lame man in Jesus' name and proclaimed the gospel to a gathering crowd, they were arrested and brought before the Sanhedrin. At this point, their lives were in danger and Peter and John had every reason to be timid, apologetic, and compliant. Instead, Peter boldly threw down the gauntlet:

> "Let me clearly state to all of you and to all the people of Israel that [the lame man] was healed by the powerful name of Jesus Christ the Nazarene, the man you crucified but whom God raised from the dead ... there is salvation in no one else!"...
>
> The members of the council were amazed when they saw the boldness of Peter and John, for they could see that they were ordinary men with no special training in the Scriptures. They also recognized them as men who had been with Jesus (Acts 4:10, 12a, 13 NLT).

The unstable, shifty Simon whom Jesus renamed in the first chapter of John (Session 1) had clearly grown into his new name and altar ego — Peter, the rock. He was an ordinary man made extraordinarily bold by knowing Christ.

- What is most challenging to you, or most encouraging to you, about Peter's boldness and his transformation?

- Craig said, "The goal is not to be bold; the goal is to know Jesus." What would you say is the potential danger when spiritual boldness *is* the goal — when it is rooted more in love of self (ego) than love of Christ (altar ego)?[8]

---

8. For a biblical example, consider the description of Peter's behavior in John 18:1 – 11.

Requesting Boldness

4. After threatening Peter and John — likely with imprisonment or
   worse — the religious leaders commanded them not to speak or
   teach in Jesus' name and then released them. When the two apostles
   shared with the other believers all that had happened, those gathered
   immediately began to pray. First, they praised God and affirmed his
   sovereignty (Acts 4:24b – 28), and then they presented their requests:

   > "And now, O Lord, hear their threats, and give us, your ser-
   > vants, great *boldness* in preaching your word. Stretch out your
   > hand with healing power; may miraculous signs and wonders
   > be done through the name of your holy servant Jesus."

   > After this prayer, the meeting place shook, and they were all
   > filled with the Holy Spirit. Then they preached the word of God
   > with *boldness* (Acts 4:29 – 31 NLT, emphasis added).

   The Greek word translated as "boldness" is significant and rich
   with meaning. In Greek culture, *parrhēsia* (par-rhay-see´-ah) was
   a defining characteristic of free speech. In civic life, Greek citizens
   had the right to freely (boldly) share their opinions, whereas non-
   citizens and slaves did not.[9] In personal relationships, *parrhēsia*
   was an expectation of conversation among friends — to trust someone was to speak openly and even bluntly when necessary.[10]

   - How might the meaning of *parrhēsia* in Greek civic life reflect
     something true about believers in the early church? For
     example, what does their prayer and boldness reveal about
     their "citizenship"? What does their ability to preach with
     boldness reveal about their relationship with God?

---

9. Hans-Christoph Hahn, "*parrhēsia*," *New International Dictionary of New Testament
   Theology*, vol. 2, Colin Brown, gen. ed. (Grand Rapids: Zondervan, 1978, 1986), 735.
10. David W. J. Gill, "1 Corinthians," *Zondervan Illustrated Bible Backgrounds
   Commentary*, vol. 3, Clinton E. Arnold, gen. ed. (Grand Rapids: Zondervan, 2002), 133.

- Perhaps as significant as what the believers ask God for is what they do *not* ask God for. Knowing that their lives are at risk, what kinds of things might you expect them to ask for? Why do you imagine they ask instead for great boldness (*parrhēsia*)?

- The believers' prayer for boldness is specific to speech — they ask for "great boldness in preaching [God's] word," and that is the prayer God answers.

  In what relationship or area of your life are you most aware of the risks or threat of talking openly about your faith? If God were to answer your prayer for great boldness, what would you want to say?

Circles of Boldness

5. The key to developing spiritual boldness — and growing into your altar ego — is spending more time with Jesus. The opposite is also true; spending less time with Jesus decreases spiritual boldness.

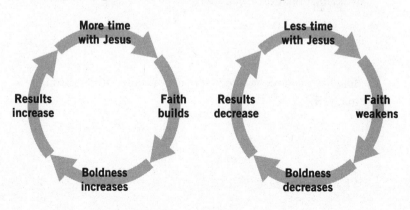

- When you reflect on your faith journey up to now, when would you say you were most intentional about investing in your relationship with Christ? For example, was it when you first became a believer, right now, or sometime between the two? How did you experience the four elements on the circle of boldness?

- Which of the two circle diagrams would you say best represents where you are right now? If you can think of any, share a recent experience that illustrates your current spiritual boldness level (high, medium, or low).

6. Reflect on and discuss what you've learned and experienced together throughout the *Altar Ego* curriculum.

  - What would you say are some of the most significant things you learned throughout the study? How has what you've learned impacted you (for example, in your attitudes, behaviors, relationships, etc.)?

  - How have you recognized God at work in your life through this study?

  - What do you sense God's invitation to you might be?

- At the end of every session, you had an opportunity to talk about what you needed from the other members of the group and how you could be good companions for one another. What changes, if any, have you noticed in the ways you interact with each other now compared to the beginning of the study?

Individual Activity: **What I Want to Remember** (2 Minutes)

1. Briefly review the outline and any notes you took.
2. In the space below, write down the most significant thing you gained in this session — from the teaching, activities, or discussions.

   What I want to remember from this session . . .

Closing Prayer

Close your time together with prayer.

Personal Study

● Read and Learn

Read chapters 9 – 12 of the *Altar Ego* book. Use the space below to note any insights or questions.

● Study and Reflect

Fear keeps our egos front and center and in need of reassurance from other people or from our possessions or titles. But when we lay our egos on the altar of belief, our altar egos become liberated to live by faith and not by fear.

Altar Ego, page 165

1. Living with spiritual boldness means living out loud — allowing what you believe to be obvious in your words as well as your actions. This makes spiritual boldness risky.

   Use the prompts that follow to reflect on any risks and fears you might have about spiritual boldness. For each item, ask yourself: *What is at risk or what am I afraid of losing in this area of life if I were to speak more boldly about my faith?*

   People: Consider your larger social circles as well as individual relationships with family, friends, colleagues, neighbors, acquaintances, etc.

Possessions: Consider anything that could be called an asset or a benefit you currently enjoy. This might include access to resources, privileges, or even a way of life.

Titles: Consider anything that gives you a sense of significance, authority, or belonging. It could be a job title but it could also be anything that routinely wins you praise or acceptance from others (a reputation for being a fun or an open-minded person, etc.).

Other: What other risks or fears come to mind?

2. Fear keeps the unredeemed ego front and center. In connection
   with spiritual boldness, it compels us to avoid anything that
   threatens our image — the idealized person we want to be and
   who we present to the world for affirmation and acceptance.

   As you review the risks and fears you wrote about in question 1,
   circle or highlight the one you think might pose the greatest threat
   to your image (your idealized self). Briefly reflect on the context
   associated with the threat you noted — the physical setting, relationships, activities, etc. Now imagine that Jesus is physically present with you in that context. How might it change your behavior?

   How does it shift your perspective to think of Jesus himself —
   rather than just talking about Jesus — as the thing you are trying
   to avoid, the threat to your image?

**God wants us to be bold, to take risks through his leading us out of our
comfort zones.**

Altar Ego, page 164

---

3. In a letter to his young colleague, Timothy, the apostle Paul acknowledged the risks associated with speaking about Christ:

    > So never be ashamed to tell others about our Lord. And don't be ashamed of me, either, even though I'm in prison for him. With the strength God gives you, be ready to suffer with me for the sake of the Good News (2 Timothy 1:8 NLT).

    Paul made a similar statement in his letter to the church at Philippi:

    > For I fully expect and hope that I will never be ashamed, but that I will continue to be bold for Christ, as I have been in the past. And I trust that my life will bring honor to Christ, whether I live or die (Philippians 1:20 NLT).

    The shame Paul identified in these passages is not merely an emotion, such as fear, but something intensely relational and antithetical to love. Imagine someone you love saying to you, "I love you, but I'm ashamed to be seen with you. No one can ever know I love you because it would make my life difficult." What would such a statement tell you about this person and what he or she values most? How would it impact the relationship?

    Based on the two passages, how would you describe Paul's perspective on what it means to truly love one another? To truly love Christ?

Just before encouraging Timothy not to be ashamed, Paul laid the foundation for spiritual boldness: "For God has not given us a spirit of fear and timidity, but of power, love, and self-discipline" (2 Timothy 1:7 NLT). Keeping in mind your responses to question 1, use the sentence starters below to reflect on what you need from God.

I need power from God to …

I need love from God to …

I need self-discipline from God to …

Spiritual boldness is not our goal; knowing Christ is our goal.... Spiritual boldness comes from knowing Christ.... I challenge you in the boldest way possible to be the real deal.... Fall so in love with God that everywhere you go, you overflow with a spiritual boldness of love and compassion that draws people to the joy of life in Christ.

Altar Ego, **pages 174, 176**

Spiritual boldness is not crazy, irrational, odd, illogical, subjective behavior. It is behavior that naturally reflects our love for Christ.

Briefly reflect on recent experiences of spiritual boldness — times you chose to speak or not speak openly about Christ. In what ways does each experience accurately reflect your love for Christ and your relationship with him right now?

● Guided Prayer

Jesus, thank you for enduring the shame of the cross because of your love for me. I want to live my faith out loud, to be bold in my love for you and the people you bring into my life. Yet I confess that there are times I am anything but bold. My fears always seem to get the better of me, especially when ...

Please lead me out of my comfort zones. I claim the promise that you have given me a spirit of power, love, and self-discipline so that I can be bold. I ask that you lead me out of my comfort zones by helping me to ...

Lord, what I want most of all is to know you better so that spiritual boldness is just a natural expression of my love for you. I am not ashamed of you. I love you with my whole heart and want everything I say and do to honor you. Amen.

Altar Ego

Becoming Who God Says You Are

Craig Groeschel

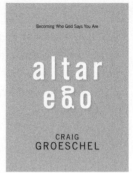

You are NOT who you think you are. In fact, according to bestselling author Craig Groeschel in *Altar Ego*, you need to take your idea of your own identity, lay it down on the altar, and sacrifice it. Give it to God. Offer it up.

Why? Because you are who GOD says you are. And until you've sacrificed your broken concept of your identity, you won't become who you are meant to be.

When we place our false labels and self-deception on the altar of God's truth, we discover who we really are as his sons and daughters. Instead of an outward-driven, approval-based ego, we learn to live with an "altar" ego, God's vision of who we are becoming.

Discover how to trade in your broken ego and unleash your altar ego to become a living sacrifice. Once we know our true identity and are growing in our Christ-like character, then we can behave accordingly, with bold behavior, bold prayers, bold words, and bold obedience.

Altar Ego reveals who God says you are, and then calls you to live up to it.

Available in stores and online!

More Popular DVD Studies from Craig Groeschel

Soul Detox

Sessions include:

1. Lethal Language: Experiencing the Power of Life-Giving Words
2. Scare Pollution: Unlocking the Chokehold of Fear
3. Radioactive Relationships: Loving Unhealthy People without Getting Sick
4. Septic Thoughts: Overcoming Our False Beliefs
5. Germ Warfare: Cleansing Our Lives of Cultural Toxins

Weird

Sessions include:

1. The God Kind of Weird
2. It's Time to Be Weird
3. Weird That Money Can't Buy
4. Pleasing God Is Weird
5. Weird Makes You Truly Sexy
6. The Weirdest Blessing Possible

The Christian Atheist

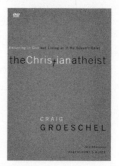

Sessions include:

1. When You Believe in God but Don't Really Know Him
2. When You Believe in God but Don't Think He's Fair
3. When You Believe in God but Aren't Sure He Loves You
4. When You Believe in God but Trust More in Money
5. When You Believe in God but Pursue Happiness at Any Cost
6. When You Believe in God but Don't Want to Go Overboard

Share Your Thoughts

With the Author: Your comments will be forwarded to the author when you send them to *zauthor@zondervan.com*.

With Zondervan: Submit your review of this book by writing to *zreview@zondervan.com*.

Free Online Resources at

www.zondervan.com

Zondervan AuthorTracker: Be notified whenever your favorite authors publish new books, go on tour, or post an update about what's happening in their lives at www.zondervan.com/authortracker.

Daily Bible Verses and Devotions: Enrich your life with daily Bible verses or devotions that help you start every morning focused on God. Visit www.zondervan.com/newsletters.

Free Email Publications: Sign up for newsletters on Christian living, academic resources, church ministry, fiction, children's resources, and more. Visit www.zondervan.com/newsletters.

Zondervan Bible Search: Find and compare Bible passages in a variety of translations at www.zondervanbiblesearch.com.

Other Benefits: Register yourself to receive online benefits like coupons and special offers, or to participate in research.

■ ZONDERVAN®

ZONDERVAN.com/
AUTHORTRACKER
follow your favorite authors